M000213733

THE
LITTLE BOOK
OF
PUTTING

T. J. Tomasi, Ph.D., is a Class A PGA teaching professional and director of the Player's School at the Academy of Golf at PGA National. Tomasi is rated by *Golf Magazine* as one of America's Top 100 teachers. One of the most widely published golf instructors in the world, he is the author of more than one hundred instructional articles for major publications such as *Golf* and *Golf Illustrated*, is a syndicated golf columnist in more than 150 cities across America, and is the author or coauthor of several books, including *The LAWs of the Golf Swing* and *Break 100 Now!* He lives in southern Florida.

THE
LITTLE BOOK
OF
PUTTING

T. J. Tomasi, Ph.D.

with John J. Monteleone

Andrews McMeel Publishing

Kansas City

A MOUNTAIN LION BOOK

Illustrations © Phil Franke

ISBN: 0-7407-1458-9

Library of Congress Catalog Card Number: 00-106921

Design and composition by Kelly & Company, Lee's Summit, Missouri

Contents

The man who can putt
is a match for anyone.

—Willie Park, three-time
British Open champion

1

Why Improve Your Putting?

In any given par-72 round, putting represents the largest category of strokes. Today's Tour pros use their putter an average of thirty times a round, approximately 43 percent of their game. From professional play to recreational golf, the flat stick is in a player's hands the greatest proportion of time. The implications of focusing your practice on putting are obvious, in fact, comparable to mining a mother lode—this is where you get the biggest payoff, where you improve your scoring the most.

The ability to putt well can take pressure off the other parts of your game, knowing that you can turn three shots—your approach and two putts—into two—

the approach and one putt. Good putting is also a great equalizer, giving you a par-saving up-and-down (holing out from off the green in two shots, one of which is normally a putt) after you've missed the green with a wayward approach shot.

Improvement in your putting comes faster than improvement in any other part of your game. You don't need superior strength, eye-hand coordination, or athleticism to improve your putting. The mechanics, setup, and body movements can be quickly mastered by golfers of every athletic ability.

Should Golfers, Even Pros, Become Irate When They Miss a Putt?

A recent study found that Tour players make only 54.8 percent of the putts attempted from six feet; they make only 33.5 percent of those from ten feet; and at fifteen feet, it gets worse—only 16.8 percent are made. However, the study found that pros tend to do better when the shot is for par compared to for a birdie. Is it the pressure of keeping up with their peers?

Practicing Is Convenient

Practicing putting is convenient and easy. For one, you don't have to pick up balls spread out over a range. You can practice on the carpet in your home as well as on a putting green. You cannot do this when practicing the full swing, even if you're hitting Wiffle balls.

Use Any Style That Works

Putting allows for idiosyncratic styles. Ben Crenshaw, one of the modern game's premier putters, once observed, "If there is one thing certain about putting, it is that it's an individual business. The great putters

Silence Is Golden— Etiquette While on the Green

Here are some helpful etiquette tips while on the green.

- *On completion of play on a hole by all players in the group, repair any damage to the putting green caused by golf shoe spikes.*
- *On entering the green, fix ball marks.*
- *Avoid stepping on the putting lines of others.*
- *When another player is putting, don't stand in his line of direct*

or peripheral vision. Keep still and quiet.

- *When retrieving a holed putt, do not flip the ball from the cup with your putter (can damage edge of cup).*

- *If you're tending the flag, don't stand near the hole or on an extension of the line behind the hole (this avoids the situation in which the putt goes beyond the hole and the second putt must then be rolled back over your footprints). Hold the flag so it doesn't flap in the breeze.*

have used every conceivable type of grip, stance, and stroke."

For example, Bobby Locke, considered one of the best putters of all time, was famous for imparting topspin on his putts with a "hooding" of the face of his putter during his backswing, while Billy Casper, another all-time great putter, rapped and tapped his putts with a snappy wrist action.

Isao Aoki, the great player from Japan, addresses and strokes the ball in an unorthodox style. He holds the toe of his blade cocked high in the air and he strokes the ball with a steep, downward motion.

But his putts pass the ultimate test: They consistently go in the hole. Like Aoki, you don't have to model yourself precisely after the great putting masters. You can learn the basics of putting from this little book and adapt these principles to your individual style and execution. That's the beauty of putting—no style points and a dearth of instructional dogma. The ultimate criteria of success is whether you can get the ball in the hole. Play away!

2

*What Is the
Essence of
Good Putting?*

The ability to putt well derives from several sources. Confidence produces good putting. The ability to accurately read greens contributes. So does the execution of proper mechanics—setup, alignment, and stroking of the ball—as does repetitious practice.

Golf immortal Bobby Jones thought a good putter was a player who consistently kept coming close. "The good putter gets his ball more times within a one-foot radius. He holes more putts because, of the greater number that come close, a greater number more likely will go in."

When you put all of these together, you've got a good start on describing what makes up good putting.

I've observed that good putters are good from the distances they putt from the most, and great putters are good from any distance. However, it all starts with realistic expectations. Good putters understand what's realistic and what's not.

For example, good putters know that when faced with a putt from six feet there's at least a fifty-fifty chance of sinking it. They try to make every one, but they know what is realistic. They play with expectations based on known statistical data and norms.

So when a good putter has a hot streak—that is, he's just drained four putts from beyond ten feet—he knows he's not going to make these putts forever.

Know and Play
by the Rules

*Here are some important rules
about what you may and may not
do while putting on the green.*

- *You may repair an old hole plug
  or damage to the putting
  green caused by the impact
  of a ball (you may do this even
  if your ball does not lie on the
  green). If the ball is moved in
  the process of repair, it shall
  be replaced without penalty.*

- *A ball on the putting green may be lifted and, if desired, cleaned. A ball so lifted shall be replaced on the spot from which it was lifted.*

- *The line of the putt may not be touched except that the player may move sand and loose soil on the putting green and other loose impediments (such as leaves) by picking them up or brushing them aside with his hand or club without pressing anything down.*

- *During the play of a hole, a player shall not test the surface of the putting green by rolling a ball or roughening or scraping the surface.*

- *A player shall not make a stroke on the putting green from a stance astride, or with either foot touching, the line of the putt or an extension of that line behind the ball. (You can't putt as if you're playing croquet!)*

- *When any part of the ball overhangs the lip of the hole, the player is allowed enough time to reach the hole without unreasonable delay and an additional twenty seconds to determine whether the ball is at rest. If by then the ball has not fallen into the hole, it is deemed to be at rest.*

When the streak cools, he's not upset. He knows he's made his "fair share," and that no one can consistently hole out from beyond ten feet. He's demonstrated good temperament and a winner's attitude;

he's kept himself on an even keel. Neither a hot streak nor the inherent vagaries of golf can drive him off his steady course.

The mechanics of good putting depend on getting the direction and distance correct. As you align your body and aim the putter face, you automatically fix the geometry of direction. Now, to produce a good putt, all that you need to do is apply the correct amount of force.

The actual mechanics of the stroke is best left to what I call "unconscious competence." This is when you leave the mind clear to imagine—see in your mind's eye—the putt. In contrast, you learn the mechanics of the your stroke by using conscious competence; that is, you learn

Proper setup and alignment include eyes along the target line.

the various elements one by one, then put them all together and no longer think of them as separate or individual movements.

When you put the elements into unconscious competence, you forget the sequences of what and how and let the overriding image drive the stroke. This is what Arnold Palmer calls the "blessed state in which you perform without knowing or giving the slightest thought to how you're performing."

If you want to consistently putt the correct distance and in the right direction, you must practice, but not mindlessly. If you care enough to improve, you must practice with intent.

Here's how. Devise a plan or scheme of practice that helps to ingrain one or more of the basic putting skills. For example, you can improve your distance control by carefully quantifying the distances of your practice putts, then calibrating and practicing the adjustments in the lengths of the strokes that each distance calls for.

Practice this simple drill. Walk off twelve paces—thirty-six feet—on a relatively flat area of the green and place a ball at each three-foot (one pace) interval. You should have twelve balls in place, the first resting at three feet from the hole and the last resting at thirty-six feet from the hole. Starting with the ball nearest the hole,

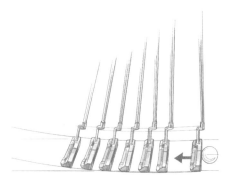

*Match the length of your takeaway
with the length of the putt.*

roll each putt toward the hole. Concentrate on learning the length of your takeaway or backswing and forward swing for each putt. Repeat this drill placing balls at distances of three feet, nine feet, fifteen feet, twenty-one feet, twenty-seven feet, and thirty-three feet and then putting each, starting with the ball placed at three feet. Repeat again placing balls at nine, twenty-one, and thirty-three feet and putting each.

Remember, when you can consistently achieve what you intended in practice, you acquire confidence. And confidence is a cornerstone of good putting.

3

What Are the Proper Grip and Setup?

Gripping the Putter

The key to developing a good putting stroke is to grip the club in such a way that it quiets the hands. Square the club-face, then set your hands on the grip with the palms facing each other and the putter face positioned square to the target line. The facing palms should be square, or perpendicular, to the target line. For a right-handed player, the palm of the right hand should be parallel to an imaginary line created by the face of the putter.

Place the grip of your putter along the lifeline of your left hand. The lifeline cuts diagonally across your left palm, angled from just left of your index finger to the

What Are the Proper Grip and Setup?

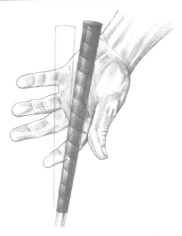

Place the putter deep in the palm.

lower right of the palm near the wrist. This puts the handle deeper in the palm than the grips taken when hitting with your other clubs and helps to eliminate wrist action.

Now check the grip. The back of your left hand should face the target. Your thumbs are on top of the handle. Your right index finger is wrapped around the handle, and the middle knuckle points down between the feet. A slight space is created on the target side of the putter shaft between the tip of the wrapped index finger and the thumb placed atop of the handle.

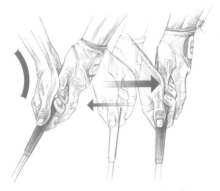

Grip the putter with the back of the left hand facing the target.

Join the Hands with a Comfortable Grip

The hands may be joined with an overlap grip, a reverse overlap grip, or an interlocking grip, or aligned alongside each other with a baseball grip (also known as a split-hands grip). With the overlap grip the pinky finger of the right hand lies over and slightly between the index and middle finger of the left hand. With the reverse overlap grip, the index finger of the left hand lies over the fingers of the right hand.

Jack Nicklaus prefers this grip because it puts the four fingers of his right hand on the handle and gives him a right-hand-dominant stroke (he advocates a stroke that pushes with his right hand along the target line).

The interlocking grip requires that the pinky finger of the right hand and the index finger wrap around each other, thus "locking" the two hands. The baseball grip aligns all fingers on the handle with no overlapping or interlocking.

Setup

Set your shoulders squarely so your arms hang straight down. Bend forward at the waist and hips till your eyes are directly over the ball or slightly behind the ball looking along an imaginary line drawn

*The hands are set slightly
forward of the ball in setup.*

through the ball along the target or aiming line.

To locate the target from this position, rotate your head. Do not lift your head; this will disrupt your eye line.

Your kinesthetic and visual systems synchronize and work with the information provided—in short, you will putt where you're looking. So how you set your eyes at address is extremely important. Setting your eyes correctly gives you the proper aiming of the putter face. If your eyes are outside your target line, that is, not directly along the target line but on the far side, you will see the hole as being left of its true position. If your eyes are inside the target line, that is, on the near side, you will see the hole as being right of its actual position.

Select Your Posture

Your posture can take one of two acceptable putting positions: (1) a more upright, less angled spine position as exemplified by Ben Crenshaw or Phil Mickelson or (2) a more angled or tilted spine position as practiced by Jack Nicklaus or Dave Stockton.

The position or tilt of the spine may vary from more upright to slightly tilted, but the forearms, when viewed from down the target line, must create and maintain a level plane. Your left forearm is directly

What Are the Proper Grip and Setup?

Align the shoulders, hips, knees, ankles, and shoe tips.

in front of the putter shaft and the right forearm is directly behind it, equidistant from the target line. If your right arm is higher, you'll have a tendency to pull your putts. If your left arm is higher, you will push your putts.

Arms Operate as Unit

The arms operate as a unit during the stroke. If you allow your forearms to roll—that is, move the right arm over the left arm as normally done when completing the follow-through of a full swing—you'll mishit your putts both left and right, depending on the early or late timing of the rolling action.

Your shoulders are parallel to the target line. If you have them closed at address your putter head swings too much from inside to out. Result? A putt pushed to the right. If your shoulders are too open, your putter head swings across the target line from right to left (outside to inside the target line). Result? A putt pulled left of the target.

Shoulder Alignment and Hand Position

Align your shoulders parallel to the target line and let your hands hang down comfortably under them. This will allow your hands and arms to ride back and forth

When stroking the ball, operate shoulders, arms, and hands as a unit.

smoothly, parallel to the target line. Should you position your hands either outside or inside the imaginary parallel line to the target line, they will automatically try to get back under your shoulders as you swing the arms, thus disrupting the intended path of your putter. When your hands are too close to the body (too far inside), you will cut putts. When the hands are too far away, you will cuff or push putts. Cuffing is an overuse of the right hand at the last second, akin to a topspin overhand movement in tennis.

If you putt from a more upright posture, keep your weight evenly distributed between the feet and anchor the weight more toward the heels. If you prefer the

How to Find the Sweet Spot of Your Putter

To find the sweet spot on your club, hold the putter by the top of its grip, between your index finger and thumb, like a plumb line. Take a golf tee and tap the face of the putter, beginning with the toe end, then the heel, and gradually zero in on the point at which the putter head swings straight back, twisting neither inward nor outward. This area is the sweet spot. Mark the center of it on the top of the blade. Years ago this spot was the size of a dime, but today it can be as large as a half-dollar.

Hit the ball on the sweet spot of the club. If you miss this spot by a quarter of an inch, 98 percent of your error will translate to the ball. For any putt longer than eight feet, this error will make you miss the cup.

tilted spine posture, favor a slight weight shift onto the front leg and toward the balls of your feet.

Place the putter directly opposite the midline or axis of your body and place the ball in front of the putter face so it almost touches your putter face. If you're putting on Bermuda grass move the ball and putter face slightly forward to put topspin on the ball.

Choosing the Right Putter

Putters come in all shapes and sizes and are made of myriad materials. However, the heads are connected either to a shaft in the middle of the blade or a shaft that is off center (anywhere between the center and the end of the putter face that is farthest from the target line). The center-shafted putters are mallets and the end-shafted putters are blades.

Heel-shafted blades are more suitable to players who have a more upright putting posture. Center-shafted mallets work better for players who putt from a more angled spine posture. The latter—what I call "benders"—have a more up-and-down shoulder motion, and thus create a more straight-back and straight-through movement of the putter face. The more upright putting posture promotes a flatter shoulder movement—one that moves "around" rather than up and down. Thus, a heel-shafted blade, which can swing open like a gate in what is called an inside-to-square-to-inside stroke, better suits the player whose putting stance is more upright.

The putter's shape must assist you in setting it absolutely square to your chosen target line. When the putter is placed so that your hands have a comfortable position on the handle, the head must rest flat behind the ball without any further manipulation of your hands, arms, shoulders, or feet.

Set Face of Putter Square to Target Line

Being able to consistently set the putter square to the target line is critical to achieving success. Consider that a deviation from a square or perpendicular setting of one degree will result in a deviation of 1.5 inches in a straight putt of 6 feet. The diameters of the cup and ball are 4.25 inches and 1.6 inches, respectively. There isn't much room for error in golf, and the closer you get to the hole the less room for error there is. Thus, any straight putts that are struck with a misaligned putter face will probably not hole out.

What's the lesson from all of this? Choose a putter that fits your setup and keep the face square to the target line at impact!

4

What Is the Proper Stroke?

The putting stroke is intrinsically linked with myriad other factors—posture, stance, hand pressure, style of putter—but there are a few absolutes that govern good putting. One link, however, between posture and stroke needs some clarification.

To be a good putter you must match your posture with your type of stroke. Generally, if you putt from a tilted spine—that is, you're bent over like Arnold Palmer—you'll putt better if you make a square-to-square, down-the-line putting stroke in which the putter face stays on line throughout. If you putt with an upright posture—like Phil Mickelson—you'll putt better if you swing the putter slightly inside on the backstroke, square it just

What Is the Proper Stroke?

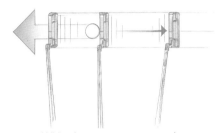

*With a bent-over posture, make
a square-to-square stroke.*

before and through the impact area, and
then bring it back inside at the end of the
follow-through.

Note that both strokes require the putter to travel down the target line, square

to the target, somewhat equal distances before impact and after impact. This is a constant, or absolute, regardless of your posture and style of stroke—the clubface must be square to the intended line of roll before impact, at the moment of impact, and shortly after.

Stroking Motion Simulates the Action of a Pendulum

I liken the action of a putting stroke to the swinging motion of a pendulum of a grandfather clock. I'm not alone in this appraisal, as many of the greatest golfers use the pendulum stroke. Seve Ballesteros, for one, feels that the key to any

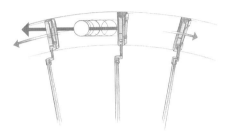

With an upright stance, use a stroke that opens, squares (at impact), and closes the blade.

successful putting stroke is "to keep a perfect pendulum action, with the club-head moving backward and forward the same distance, at the same speed."

What do you have to do to achieve a pendulum motion? Take your stance, arms hanging freely directly under your shoulders. Grip the club and take notice of the angle at the wrist joint created by the back of the right hand and lower arm. You must keep this angle intact throughout your putting stroke.

Place your eyes over the ball or behind it along the target line. Think of the top of your spine as an anchor point around which your shoulders will gently rock. Make a one-piece stroke with everything (hands, arms, and putter head) moving together while you keep the top of your spine— the anchor—completely motionless.

Keep the Triangle Shape Formed by Your Arms at Address

This one-piece takeaway allows your arms to rock softly while maintaining the triangle formed at address by your arms and shoulders. Maintain an equal distance between the elbows, and avoid hinging the wrists. This will provide a constant distance for the bottom of the putting arc, a key for striking the ball squarely and solidly. To maintain the putter face square along the target line, keep the hands facing each other on the grip by applying soft but firm pressure against each other.

With the pendulum action the clubhead will be moving fastest at the lowest point due to gravity. Don't try to add speed. This tends to open the clubface. Never slow down the putter as you approach the ball. This happens most often when you make a backstroke that is too long, and it tends to shut the clubface, causing putts to move off line to the left.

Here are a couple more things to avoid.

- Don't manipulate the putter; that is, don't add or subtract any energy as the clubface squares along the target line. With the correct stroking motion, there is no "hit." Rather, your clubface, helped by momentum and

As you rock the shoulders, keep the triangle throughout the stroke.

Should You Put a Little Extra on Your Putts?

Some say "Yes," and others say "No." Short-game guru Dave Pelz says that you should putt a ball so that if the hole were covered, the putt would roll seventeen inches past the hole. This speed enables the ball to hold its line through what Pelz calls the "lumpy dough-nut." As Pelz describes it, most of the green is marked up and stamped down from footprints, except the last foot before the cup, which is smooth because golfers make a point to keep off that area.

Thus, as a ball makes its way toward the cup, it must contend with depressions as deep as one-eighth inch (or 7½ percent of the ball's height) until it is a foot from the cup. Then the ball actually has to run up a little ramp when it is going slowly and is least prepared to do so. Pelz says this explains why so many putts veer off or stop short at the last second.

On the other hand, golfing legend Bobby Jones advocated

reaching the hole with a dying ball. He felt that when the ball dies at the hole, it has four doors it can go in: the front, back, and either side, wherever it touches the rim. But a ball that comes up to the hole with speed on it must hit the front door in the middle.

Jones also felt that the maxim "Never up, never in," which urged players to always leave the ball beyond the hole, led to too many three-putt greens. "For my part, I have holed more long putts when trying to reach the cup with a

dying ball than by 'gobblin' or
hitting hard. If the dying ball
touches the rim, it usually drops.
And if it doesn't touch the rim—
well, you can usually cover the
hole and the ball with a hat,
which makes your next putt
simple and keeps down the
strain."

So there you have it—two
schools of thought on the approach
putt: (1) Hit it past the hole or
(2) hit it just up to the hole, on
any one of four sides. Take your
choice!

gravity, is naturally accelerating at impact.

- Don't put a "death grip" on the handle. This creates tension, which decreases your ability to control the rhythm of your putting stroke and ultimately the direction in which the putter faces at impact (it must be square to the target upon contact).

Pop-Piston Putting Style— Easy to Learn

Slower greens predominated on most American golf courses forty to fifty years ago. To putt effectively on these greens players employed the "pop" stroke, a wristy motion that literally propelled the ball through the air for a short distance (putters have loft, too) and then imparted a forward rotation of the ball when it returned to the green. Many greens today, especially those on the courses played by touring pros, are cut shorter and more evenly and don't require this type of compensating stroke. However, today's recreational golfers don't always have access to these smooth-as-glass surfaces and more often play on greens that are slower and bumpier.

In order to play more effectively, and score better, on these greens, you might try putting with a blend of yesteryear's pop

When You Hit a Poor Putt, Watch It All the Way

When you hit a poor putt, whether it is long or short of the hole, do not turn your head away in disgust. As long as the ball is within five feet of the hole, pay attention to what it does as it runs by or comes up short of the hole.

Why? You have a short putt remaining to be played—a putt that will not require much speed. When the ball is moving slowly, it is more susceptible to break. In fact, it is showing you the exact amount of break the ball is going to take on the next putt.

So stay focused and pay close attention to the entire roll of the approach putt. A putt that barely misses the hole and rolls by is a preview of the putt returning—the one you need to put it in the hole.

style and today's quiet wrist, shoulder-dominant style. I call it the Pop-Piston stroke. It is not a true pendulum stroke, but a variation. It is easy to learn, and best of all—it will give you consistency and success with your putts.

Begin by positioning the ball forward, more toward the left toe (for a right-handed golfer). Open your stance slightly. This accommodates the forward ball position. Position your eyes slightly behind the ball but directly along the line of the putt.

Place your thumbs on top of the handle and your left index finger along the outside of your right hand on the left side of the shaft. Distribute your weight so that it favors your target foot. Anchor your right elbow against the right hip.

Backstroke

Then as you begin the pendulum motion push the clubhead back with this finger, keeping your right elbow fixed to the right hip just as it was at address. This will keep the putter head from moving off your target line. The amount of push by the left index finger should match the amount you deem necessary to roll the putt the required distance.

At the end of your backstroke, your right wrist should be cupped; look for wrinkles on the back of your wrist. Your left wrist remains unhinged and straight; that is, if you were to draw a line from the back of your left wrist toward your elbow, it would be perfectly straight. The putter face is square to the target line.

Forward Stroke

After you've fully cocked the putter, use your right palm (as if it were a piston) to shove the entire assembly—hands, arms, and putter head—forward, applying the force necessary to roll the ball to the target. The left wrist stays straight; the right wrist stays cupped. The arms maintain the bend or angle taken at address.

This combination putting stroke—using the pop-style backstroke and a shoulder-dominant forward stroke—cap-

The Pop-Piston stroke maintains a straight left wrist throughout.

tures the best performance attributes of each style. The pop action of the back-stroke, regardless of its length, better enables you to keep the putter head square to the line and continually along your intended line. This is because the power of the Pop-Piston stroke doesn't come from the length of the backswing, but rather from the force of the piston push of the forward stroke.

The shoulder-forward stroke enables you to maintain acceleration and strike the ball in the center of the putter face. And it provides the same benefits of the popular shoulder stroke—the putter face remains square to the line throughout the stroke.

The Importance of Being Square

Should you strike a twenty-foot putt ten degrees from square to the target, the ball will miss the hole by about three feet.

Good Distance

After you have chosen the line on which you wish to roll your putt, take a practice stroke next to your ball looking at the hole. This will allow your mind to program the distance of the putt. Your eyes gather the distance information and transmit it to the brain. The brain then calculates how much energy is required when you stroke the putt.

For an uphill putt, take your practice swing farther from the hole. This will help adjust for the added force you'll need to run the ball up the slope. If you're facing a downhill putt stand closer to the hole to program hitting a putt with less force.

Drills for Distance Control

Drill No. 1. Place three shafts or golf clubs on a practice green at ten-foot intervals from your ball. Putt the first ball to the shaft farthest from you, approximately thirty feet. Putt the second ball to the middle shaft, twenty feet away. Putt the third ball to the shaft closest to you, about ten feet away.

Drill No. 2. Position yourself in the middle of a practice green with a dozen balls. Pick a spot on the edge of the green and putt to it, trying not to roll the ball on the fringe. Continue clockwise with the remainder of the balls until you've putted around the twelve hourly positions on the imaginary clockface.

A Putting Routine

A putting routine isn't a mindless ritual, but rather a specific, directive process

A Pre-Putt Routine:
It's as Simple as 1, 2, 3, 4, 5

Here is a foolproof way to ritualize your putting setup, synchronize your stroke, and put rhythm (while reducing tension) in your routine.

1. *Take a practice stroke looking at the ball, then slide your putter forward so that the sweet spot is directly behind the ball and the putter is square to the target line.*

2. Set your feet in position and count "one thousand one" as you look down the line to the hole.

3. Bring your eyes back to the ball on "one thousand two."

4. On "one thousand three" draw back your putter.

5. On "one thousand four" bring the putter back along the target line through the ball.

Look at your putt from three different points.

to help you locate the target and let your brain get the distance and direction right by feeding its "need to know." Obviously, this makes the putting routine a crucial part of the overall shot. Here's what to do.

Use what I call "triangulation" to nail down the exact position of the cup and how to get the ball there. Triangulation involves viewing your putt from three different vantage points. If you're currently using only one vantage point, such as from behind the ball, you're likely to encounter parallax—the distortion or displacement of an observed object (the target) owing to a change in the position of the observer, such as when you tilt your head to putt after viewing the ball from a level-headed position of the eyes. Watch a surveyor at a road construction site. He'll make his measurements from at least two different positions, since he can't afford to be fooled. Neither can you. The next time you're on the green, survey your putt from these three positions:

1. From behind the hole
2. From behind the ball
3. From midway to the hole on the low side of the slope

Notice that as you move from point to point, you create a triangle around the hole. From each point on the triangle, you'll find yourself altering your predictions of how the ball will track toward the hole and changing your target accordingly. Moving between each of the three different vantage points forces your brain to recalculate the location of the target. Don't become uncomfortable with this changing mental state of affairs—the more data that your brain processes, the more likely it is to get the exact location right.

The process of triangulation supplies you with information as to where the hole is located and the direction your ball will travel. All that's left to do is for you to roll the putt.

5

How to Read the Green

Never Up,
Never In

Here is a tip to help you hole those short putts. When you can see into the hole from your address position, pick a spot on the back of the cup liner and putt to it as your target. This increases your accuracy by forcing you to focus on a smaller target, one you can miss—or come up slightly short of—and still make.

Reading the green is an acquired skill that anyone can learn. You have to know what to look for and how to apply the information and clues that you gather.

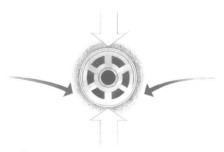

The effects of grain are magnified around the cup where the ball is slowing down.

For one thing, the way an architect designs a putting green helps you evaluate the effects of a green. Look for drainage patterns that draw water off to the sides away from the center of the green. Look for changes in the coloring of the grass surrounding the green and damage from past accumulations of water—these are clues as to how the water flows off and away from the greens, and ultimately how the ball will roll when you putt.

Grain is the prevailing direction in which the grass blades are growing. When you roll a putt directly into the ends of the blades—that is, against the grain—the blades of grass cause friction. When grain grows in the downgrade direction of a slope it can increase the break significantly. The grain of the grass will point toward any body of water that's nearby and it will always point down the slope—in the direction that the water flows. Rolling a putt up a slope means having to hit the ball uphill and against the grain—factors that mean you must greatly increase the force of the stroke.

If the grain runs across the line of your putt in the same direction as the slope of the green, it will have little effect while the ball maintains its speed but it will increase the break as the ball slows down.

Types of Grass

Bermuda grass—more often found on greens in tropical climates—grows toward the setting sun. It is thick and grows in an upward swirl. Generally, you must stroke putts on greens of Bermuda grass more firmly—especially if you want to hole the three- and four-foot finishing putts.

Bent grass—grown in cooler climates—lies down as it grows and its grain is not as severe. It grows toward natural supplies of water and away from the heights of mountains or hills.

Read 'Em and Reap

Here are some guidelines for reading the greens correctly.

- The greater the slope, the more the ball's roll will be affected.
- The faster the ball speed, the less the effect of the slope.
- The closer the cut of the grass (a faster green), the more the slope will affect the putt (because there is less friction).
- Downhill putts reduce the effective distance because gravity pulls the ball farther than if the ground were level.

- Uphill putts add to the effective distance of the putt compared to a level putt because gravity pushes against the ball.
- A slope near the origination of the putt will have less effect than when the slope is near the hole.
- When confronted with rolling a putt over multiple slopes, pay more attention to the slope nearest the hole because this slope will have a greater effect (as the ball slows down it will be influenced more).